Merry Christmas Jedediah
Love Mimi & Grampy
"2006"

The Very First CHRISTIANS

PAUL L. MAIER
ILLUSTRATED BY FRANCISCO ORDAZ

CPH
SAINT LOUIS

While Christmas and Easter celebrate how Christianity was born, the Church's third great festival, Pentecost, salutes its remarkable spread across the ancient world. Since this third part is often missing in books for the young, these pages should help fill the gap.

As in the companion books, *The Very First Christmas* and *The Very First Easter*, the setting is in America's western mountains, where a family's secluded location has prevented their bright 12-year-old son from attending Sunday school regularly. His grandfather answers questions that he—and perhaps many like him—have about how the *very first* Christians spread their faith. Parents may wish to explain any words, phrases, or events that go beyond the understanding of younger children.

Paul L. Maier

Text copyright © 2001 by Paul L. Maier
Illustrations copyright © 2001 by Francisco Ordaz

Published by Concordia Publishing House
3558 S. Jefferson Avenue, St. Louis, MO 63118-3968
Manufactured in the United States of America

1 2 3 4 5 6 7 8 9 10   10 09 08 07 06 05 04 03 02 01

Christopher was fishing with his grandfather at Parson's Pond, a jewel of a lake in the Rockies. Grandpa was a professor who knew as much about fishing as ancient history.

"Now watch that bobber, Chris," he warned. "The moment it dips, jerk your pole up and you may snag a trout."

"Grandpa," asked Chris. "What kind of fish is that over your license plate?"

"Oh that," Grandpa laughed. "That's a Christian symbol, just like the cross. The first Christians told about their faith in just eight words: *Jesus Christ is Son of God and Savior.* They strung together the first letter of each word, and that spells 'fish' in Greek."

"Who were the very first Christians?" asked Chris.

"Oh, that's *quite* a story, Chris," Grandpa said as he smiled. "A *great* story, in fact. Want to hear it?"

"Sure!" Christopher nodded, enthusiastically.

Leaning back, Grandpa began. "Before He ascended, Jesus told His disciples to wait in Jerusalem for the Holy Spirit to come upon them. And wait they did.

"Fifty days after the first Easter—that's why the event is called Pentecost, which means 'fifty'—the Holy Spirit *did* arrive. A great wind whistled through the room where they were gathered and flames appeared above each of their heads."

"*What?!*" exclaimed Chris. "Didn't their hair catch on fire?"

"Well, hair is the *only* part of the human body that *can* catch fire— but not this time. What's more, they all started speaking in foreign languages they had never learned."

"But ... why? It must have sounded like a madhouse!"

"Exactly!" Grandpa chuckled. "People thought they were drunk. But Peter explained to the gathering crowd that they were not. And those foreign languages would help them tell people in other countries about Jesus."

"That makes sense," Chris nodded.

"Then Peter boldly told the crowd about how Jesus—crucified, dead, and buried—had truly risen from the grave."

"Wow!" said Chris. "Did the people ... believe Peter?"

"You bet they did! About 3,000 believed and were baptized. Later on, at the gates of the temple, Peter and John healed a man who had been crippled from birth. People were so impressed—St. Luke tells us in the book of Acts—that soon there were 5,000 Christians."

"Awesome!" said Chris. "There were *that* many so quickly?"

"There were indeed, and that's no fish story!" said Grandpa, grinning. "Even a pagan Roman historian named Tacitus reports that only one generation later '*a vast multitude* of Christians' were in Rome—1,500 miles away! Those very first Christians had an *explosive* start—because the Holy Spirit was powerfully at work, building the Church."

"But what about Jesus' enemies in Jerusalem? How did they feel about what was going on?"

Grandpa went on to tell about how angry they were, and how they arrested the disciples and put them in prison—not once but *several* times, and each time they were miraculously set free. They were warned *not* to teach about Jesus, but they kept right on proclaiming Him as the risen Messiah.

"Then there was an extraordinary man named Stephen. He was one of seven deacons in the early church—men who helped take care of the poor. He taught about Christ so powerfully that he was arrested and dragged before the Council in Jerusalem—the same Council that had condemned Jesus."

"And did he escape too?"

"No," Grandpa shook his head. "Stephen became the first martyr of the church—someone who gave up his own life for what he believed. He accused the Council of opposing God and killing Christ, so they seized Stephen and *stoned* him to death."

Chris shook his head and asked, "Why Stephen ... when the other apostles went free?"

"Well, Chris, they *didn't* all go free. James, the brother of John, also gave up his life for the faith. Others would follow."

"But why did *any* of them have to be killed?"

"Death was no tragedy for them, Chris. They knew they were going on to be with Jesus in heaven. And this first persecution had some wonderful results: when Christians fled Jerusalem, they spread their faith everywhere."

Grandpa smiled, then added, "But not all the new believers were top quality! A weird fellow named Simon the Magician actually tried to *buy* the power to do miracles from Simon Peter."

"Uh-oh," muttered Chris.

"You've got it. Peter told him, 'You and your silver be *doomed!*'"

"By the way," Grandpa continued. "We've been talking about *thousands* added to the early church, but even *one* new believer is important. Weren't you proud of that first fish we caught, even though it was only one?"

"You *bet!*"

"Philip would agree. He was a deacon, just like Stephen. One day he met an officer of the Queen of Ethiopia who was reading a scroll by the prophet Isaiah, while riding in his carriage. He asked Philip to ride along with him and explain certain passages. Philip showed how they referred to Jesus as the Messiah, although written more than 700 years earlier. The officer believed and was baptized. He was only *one* convert, but that was the beginning of the conversion of Africa! Today there are more than *340 million* Christians there!"

"So even a tiny number like one *is* important!"

"It is in God's sight. Take Cornelius, for example. He was a Roman centurion and even though he was *not* a Jew, Peter brought him the Good News of salvation. He believed—*one* person, but today there are about *two thousand million* Gentile Christians!"

"Awesome!" Chris exclaimed. He had almost forgotten about fishing, the pole still tight in his hands. "But Grandpa, what about St. Paul? I've heard Mom and Dad talk about him."

"His story is *really* interesting. His original name was Saul and he actually *persecuted* the first Christians. Then one day, on his way to Damascus, something amazing happened. He was struck down on the roadway by a bright light. He heard a voice say, *'Saul, Saul, why are you persecuting Me?'* He asked, 'Who are you?' and the voice replied, *'I am Jesus, whom you are persecuting.'*"

"Oh, man! *That* must have been quite a shock!"

"It *was!* Saul was blinded and had to be led into Damascus. But there, a Christian named Ananias told him that Jesus had chosen *him* to bring the Gentile world to faith. His sight was restored and he was baptized."

"So the Christians lost an enemy and gained a powerful friend!"

"Exactly," Grandpa agreed.

"After years of study, Saul and another Christian leader named Barnabas left for a long mission journey. First they sailed to Cyprus, where they met the governor of the island and won him for the faith. From then on, Saul became known as Paul—a name more familiar to people at the time.

"Then they sailed to Asia Minor—we call it Turkey today—where they proclaimed Christ and started churches. But it wasn't always easy. In a place called Lystra, where they performed miracles, the townspeople were so impressed that they seriously thought—get this—that Paul and Barnabas were actually their false Greek gods, Hermes and Zeus!"

"You can't be serious!" Chris chuckled.

"It's true! The priests started preparing a great festival in their honor, but Paul couldn't have *that!* He quickly set them straight by telling about the *true* God. The pagan crowds now got angry and stoned Paul to death."

"*What?!*"

"Well, that's what they thought anyway. Paul was only knocked unconscious. After he came to, they left to start churches elsewhere. Then they returned to Antioch and that was the end of 'Paul's First Mission Journey.'"

"There were more?" asked Chris, keeping an eye on his bobber.

"Yes, but before the next one could begin, *the* most important church council ever held took place in Jerusalem. Some very strict Jewish Christians blamed Paul for welcoming Gentiles into the church without converting them to Judaism first. The Council had to decide if Paul was right or wrong."

"What about Peter?" Chris wondered. "Wouldn't he back St. Paul? Didn't he baptize that Cornelius fellow?"

"Right you are, lad. Peter *did* support Paul, and the Council—thank God—came down on Paul's side. James, who was Jesus' half-brother and the leader of the Council, wrote a letter to the new churches announcing this decision."

"But why was this ... Jerusalem Council so important?"

"Today Christianity is 99 percent Gentile, Chris. What if the Council had decided the other way?"

"Oh." Then Chris shouted, "*Oh!*" His fishing pole was dipping and he reeled in a three-pound rainbow trout. While proudly unhooking his catch, Chris really seemed more interested in what had happened 2000 years ago.

"Tell me about Paul's next mission journey, Grandpa," he said.

"This time Silas, another missionary, joined Paul. First they visited the new churches founded in the First Journey. At Lystra, a young man named Timothy joined them. And just before they headed to Greece, Luke joined them too."

"You mean the same Luke who wrote the Gospel *and* the Book of Acts?"

"The very same! They all sailed to a place called Philippi. There they found a group of women who worshiped God by a riverside. One of them named Lydia even invited the traveling missionaries into her home.

"Then Paul cured a slave girl who had earned lots of money through demonic fortune-telling. Her angry owners had Paul and Silas beaten and thrown into prison. Around midnight, an earthquake shook the prison, flinging open the cells and shattering their chains. The jailer in charge tried to kill himself, but Paul told him to stop. He then told him the Good News about Jesus Christ. The jailer and his whole family believed and were baptized. When the missionaries were released, they traveled westward to Thessalonica, and then turned south to Athens."

"Athens?" Chris asked. "We learned all about Athens in school: the great acropolis, the beautiful Parthenon temple—"

"Paul saw it all. He also noticed that Athens was full of other pagan temples, and he even saw an altar dedicated 'TO THE UNKNOWN GOD.' Did he ever use *that* to his advantage! He stood on Mars Hill—that's just below the Parthenon—and delivered a famous address telling the philosophers and government officials just *who* that 'unknown god' was. Some of them came to faith, and the conversion of Athens was underway. Today almost *all* Athenians are Christian."

"I'll bet Paul stayed in Athens a *long* time. *I* would have!"

"No, he went 60 miles west to Corinth, where the Romans had moved the Greek capital. In Acts, chapter 18, Luke says Paul was so successful there that leaders in the synagogue accused him of violating their law. But Gallio, the Roman governor, saw that this was Jewish law, not Roman, so he threw the case out of court—a big victory for Christianity."

"So Paul was set free?"

"Immediately! You know, Chris, if you ever get to Greece and explore the archaeological excavations at ancient Corinth, you can see the *very place* where Paul stood."

Grandpa paused, then asked, "Should I go on with Paul's Third Mission Journey, or shall we go back and clean our fish?"

"No! Let's go on."

"This time Paul headed for Ephesus, the most important city in Asia Minor—but also the cult capital of the world. It was crawling with magicians, sorcerers, exorcists, fortune-tellers, and even witches."

"All weirdos! But *why* would St. Paul want to spend time in ... an awful place like *that?*"

"He *loved* challenges, Chris. And his teaching was so powerful that the new believers there collected all their magic scrolls and occult paraphernalia and burned them to ashes. That junk was worth 50,000 pieces of silver!

"And speaking of silver, a fellow named Demetrius was getting rich by producing little silver models of the great Artemis temple at Ephesus and hawking them to visitors. But sales had fallen off with Paul in town. So Demetrius called a meeting of the silversmiths' guild in the great theater at Ephesus."

"Have archaeologists discovered that one too?"

"They didn't have much to do. It was never buried and it still stands there—24,000 seats and all!"

"Anyway," Grandpa continued, "the silversmiths shouted themselves hoarse for *two hours*, yelling, 'GREAT IS ARTEMIS OF THE EPHESIANS!' The rioters would have lynched Paul, but the city manager of Ephesus finally dismissed the crowd."

"Paul certainly knew how to get out of nasty situations!"

"Not always. At the close of his Third Mission Journey, Paul arrived in Jerusalem and was welcomed by the apostles. But ..." Grandpa shook his head sadly and continued, "some strict troublemakers among the Jewish Christians grumbled that Paul was neglecting God's Old Testament laws. The apostles knew it wasn't true, but to show that he observed the Law, Paul joined in a ceremony at the temple.

"Then disaster struck. Some of Paul's opponents from Ephesus were also at the temple. When they saw Paul, they started yelling *'Here is the man who is ruining Judaism!'*

"A terrible riot broke out in the temple courtyard as the news spread. A furious crowd started beating Paul and would probably have killed him had the Romans not saved him."

"The *Romans?*"

"Yes! The Roman fortress overlooked the temple courtyard. The officer in charge rescued Paul, found out that he was a Roman citizen, and sent him under guard to Caesarea. There he went on trial before the Roman governor, Felix. Paul made a strong defense for himself in court, but Felix sat on the case and left Paul in prison for two years."

"Two *years?*"

Grandpa nodded. "Then Felix was called back to Rome and a man named Festus replaced him. But Festus was new on the job, and lamely suggested that Paul return to Jerusalem for trial. Paul refused—it would have meant certain death—so he appealed his case to the emperor Nero."

"*Nero?!* I've heard nothing but *bad* things about him," Chris said. "Why would Paul ever do *that?*"

"The first years of Nero's rule were excellent because a great philosopher was running the government for him: Aeneas Seneca. And guess who Seneca's brother was ..."

"I have no idea ..."

"Gallio—the judge who had set Paul free in Corinth!" Grandpa could almost hear the wheels turning in Chris's head.

"*Good move, Paul!*" Chris shouted. "He appeals his case to the *brother* of the fellow who set him free!"

"Precisely! One day, Agrippa—the great-grandson of Herod the Great—and his sister Bernice paid a state visit to Festus. Again Paul made a brilliant defense of the faith."

"But now he and Luke set sail for Rome. The first half of their voyage was smooth, but then northerly headwinds grew stronger, so they sailed along the south shore of Crete, using the island as a windshield.

"When they put in at a little port called Fair Havens," Grandpa continued, "Paul warned them *not* to sail any farther, since the stormy winter season was approaching. They should have listened, but they ignored Paul and set sail again. Soon a *terrible* storm blew in from the northeast, which threatened to sink the ship and all its passengers and crew.

"They tossed the cargo overboard, but the howling winds and crashing waves raged on for 14 horrible days. Everyone onboard gave up hope, except for Paul. He announced that they would all survive, although the ship itself would be torn apart."

"How's *that* possible?" Chris wondered.

"The ship broke up in the surf off the island of Malta, but all 276 passengers were able to wade safely onto shore. After spending three winter months on the island, they set sail for Italy in early spring on another ship."

"No storm *this* time, I hope!"

"No. It was a velvet voyage all the way up to their dock in the Bay of Naples. From there they traveled to Rome over the famous Appian Way. Even before reaching Rome, they were greeted by two delegations of Roman Christians. But Paul had to wait *another* two years in Rome before the emperor heard his case."

"That's terrible," Chris objected "*Why?*"

"Because Nero wasn't in Rome at that time. Still, Paul didn't have to stay in prison. He lived in his own rented house where he taught both Jews and Gentiles quite freely, even under guard. And during that time he wrote many of his famous letters to the new churches, the ones we still read in church."

Chris almost hated to ask. "But ... what finally happened to St. Paul?"

"He was probably set free and took a fourth mission journey—first to Spain, then back to the eastern Mediterranean. But there he was arrested again and returned to Rome. And this time he ... he gave his very life for his Lord ... after living one of the greatest lives ever lived."